THREE THIEVES
BOOK SEVEN

The Iron Hand

Kids Can Press gratefully acknowledges the financial support of the Government of Ontario, through the Ontario Media Development Corporation; the Ontario Arts Council; the Canada Council for the Arts; and the Government of Canada, through the CBF, for our publishing activity.

Published in Canada and the U.S. by Kids Can Press Ltd.
25 Dockside Drive, Toronto, ON M5A 0B5

Kids Can Press is a Corus Entertainment Inc. company

www.kidscanpress.com

Edited by Yasemin Uçar
Designed by Scott Chantler and Michael Reis
Pages lettered with Blambot comic fonts

Printed and bound in Buji, Shenzhen, China, in 6/2016 by WKT Company

CM 16 0 9 8 7 6 5 4 3 2 1
CM PA 16 0 9 8 7 6 5 4 3 2 1

Library and Archives Canada Cataloguing in Publication

Chantler, Scott, author, artist
        The iron hand / Scott Chantler.

(Three thieves book 7)
ISBN 978-1-77138-052-2 (bound)   ISBN 978-1-77138-053-9 (pbk.)

        1. Graphic novels. I. Title. II. Series: Chantler, Scott.
Three thieves ; bk. 7.

PN6733.C53I76 2016   j741.5'971   C2015-907226-3

THREE THIEVES
BOOK SEVEN

The Iron Hand

SCOTT CHANTLER

Kids Can Press

ACT ONE

The Knight of Swords

I KNOW HOW YOU FEEL, DESSA.

BUT YOU SHOULDN'T BLAME YOURSELF.

7

FRIEND OF YOURS?

HE'S BEEN CHASING US SINCE WE FLED KINGSBRIDGE, TRYING TO BRING US BACK TO THE GALLOWS.

BUT HOW DID HE GET HERE?

ANOTHER SHIP, I RECKON. FOUND 'IM FLOATIN' ON A BROKEN PIECE OF ITS RAIL.

WE'LL THROW HIM BACK IF YOU WANT, DESSA...

...BUT I DON'T THINK YOU NEED WORRY ABOUT A SHARK WITH A BROKEN FIN.

YOU KNOW MY NAME NOW.

YOUR **BROTHER** TOLD ME.

YOU'VE SEEN JARED? WHERE? WHEN?

GREYFALCON TOLD ME HE WAS DEAD!

GREYFALCON IS A TRAITOR TO THE THRONE, AND A LIAR.

STUPIDLY, I TOOK JARED RIGHT TO HIM---

"WE WERE CHASING YOU TO ASTAROTH. I WASN'T EXPECTING GREYFALCON TO BE ABOARD.

"BUT WHEN HE SAW YOUR BROTHER, HE ORDERED THE REST OF THE QUEEN'S DRAGONS TO FINISH ME.

IS THAT WHAT YOU TOLD YOURSELF WHILE YOU WERE SWINGING ONE OF THESE AT MY HEAD IN THE PODHU HEALERS' TOWER?

I WAS NOT MYSELF THEN.

I ALLOWED MY GUILT OVER THE KING'S DEATH TO DISTORT MY SENSE OF DUTY.

I WAS WRONG.

I WAS, TOO.

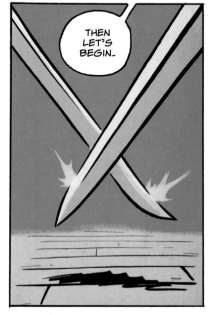

THEN LET'S BEGIN.

16

25

27

ACT TWO

The Queen and King of Crowns

"A RED CLOAK WAS LEFT BEHIND AT THE SCENE OF YOUR ABDUCTION. THE CLOAK OF ONE OF QUEEN MAGDA'S DRAGONS."

THAT'S RIGHT. WE HAVEN'T FORGOTTEN *YOU*, DRAKE.

WE CALL YOU THE BUTCHER OF BARTHELEMY FIELD.

IT WAS THERE THAT YOU GAVE ME *THIS*.

PERHAPS YOU DON'T EVEN REMEMBER.

I DO.

YOU FOUGHT HONORABLY, AND WELL. I'M NOT SURPRISED TO FIND YOU'VE BEEN PROMOTED SO HIGHLY.

DON'T WASTE YOUR SILVER TONGUE ON *ME*, VILLAIN!

YOU CAN'T WALK INTO CAMP WITH THE CROWN PRINCE, MISSING THESE PAST EIGHT WINTERS, AND PRETEND YOU DIDN'T—

HE'S GONE.

YOUR
HIGHNESS....?

HE'S
GONE.

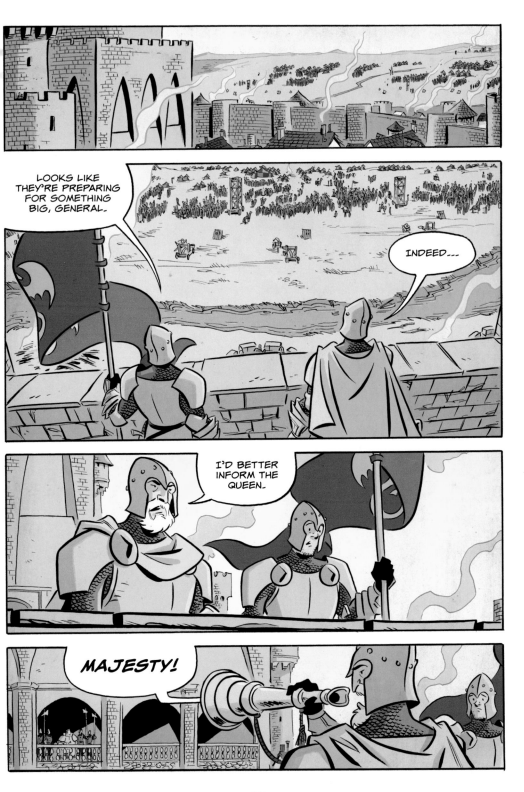

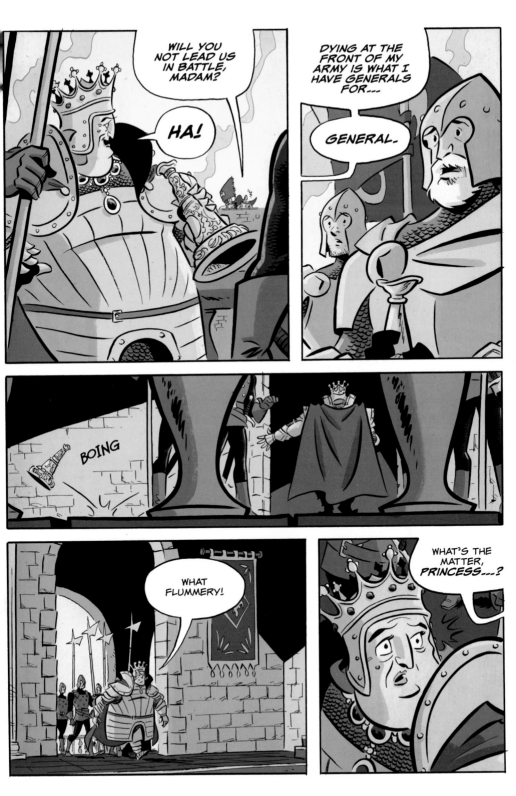

51

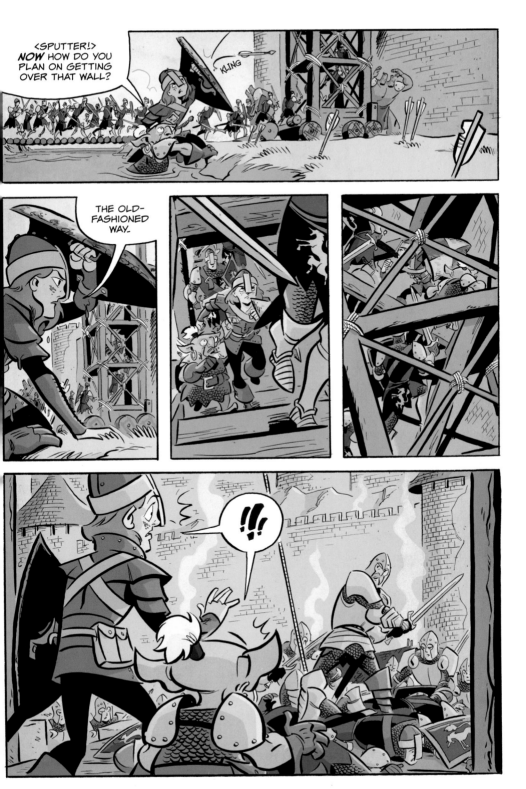

55

WHUMP

TOPPER!

<GASP!>

64

66

67

ACT THREE

The Hanged Man

"THERE CAN BE NO HARM *NOW*, I SUPPOSE, IN TELLING YOU HOW WE ENDED UP HERE.

"DID YOU EVER WONDER HOW NORTH HUNTINGTON GOT ITS NAME?

"THERE WAS ONCE A *SOUTH* HUNTINGTON, WHICH WAS ANNEXED MORE THAN HALF A CENTURY AGO...

"...WHEN RODERICK'S FATHER, KING ELGIN, WAS ON THE THRONE.

"ELGIN WAS A POPULAR MONARCH, AND NORTH HUNTINGTON A PROSPEROUS KINGDOM IN THOSE DAYS.

"THE PEOPLE OF SOUTH HUNTINGTON WERE ONLY TOO GLAD TO JOIN THEM.

"ALL BUT *TWO*, THAT IS.

"CLAN GREYFALCON HAD BEEN ON THE THRONE OF SOUTH HUNTINGTON SINCE THE AVATAR HIMSELF WALKED THE EARTH.

"MY BROTHER AND I HAD BEEN NEXT IN LINE.

"TWO FUTURE KINGS ROBBED OF THEIR HERITAGE, MADE LESSER NOBLES OVERNIGHT.

"THE PEOPLE OF OUR FORMER KINGDOM MIGHT WELL HAVE BEEN PROUD TO HAVE SUCH AN INDUSTRIOUS PAIR OF ITS SONS WEAR CROWNS.

"AT AN EARLY AGE, I DEVELOPED A PROFOUND INTEREST IN *MACHINES.*

"WHILE MOST SIMPLETONS LACKED THE IMAGINATION TO DO MUCH EXCEPT PULL THEM BEHIND ANIMALS, I BEGAN TO ENVISION HOW THEY MIGHT PRODUCE MORE....

"...*DRAMATIC* RESULTS.

"MY BROTHER RYLAN WAS SIMILARLY GIFTED. BUT HIS INCLINATIONS RAN MORE TOWARD TOYS AND TRINKETS.

"WHEN IT WAS TIME FOR US TO MAKE OUR OWN WAY IN THE WORLD, MY ABILITIES QUICKLY CAME TO THE ATTENTION OF THE IRON HAND, THE FEARED BROTHERHOOD OF ASSASSINS.

"SO I TURNED TO WHERE MY TALENTS WOULD BE APPRECIATED.

"THIS WORK BROUGHT ME TO KINGSBRIDGE, THE ROYAL CITY...

"...WHERE ELGIN'S SON RODERICK NOW RULED.

"MY ROYAL BLOOD, HOWEVER LESSENED, WAS ENOUGH FOR ME TO GAIN ADMISSION TO RODERICK'S COURT.

"FROM THERE, I BOWED AND SCRAPED MY WAY INTO HIS INNER CIRCLE.

"IMPRESSED WITH WHAT HE CALLED MY 'FASTIDIOUSLY ORDERED MIND,' THE KING EVENTUALLY APPOINTED ME HIS CHAMBERLAIN...

"A POSITION WHICH PUT ME IN CHARGE OF THE ENTIRE ROYAL HOUSEHOLD...

"INCLUDING ITS *TREASURY.*

"I DO NOT REMEMBER PRECISELY WHEN I DECIDED THAT HE MUST DIE.

"PERHAPS THE IDEA HAD ALWAYS BEEN WITH ME.

"BUT IT BECAME CLEAR THAT IF I COULD NOT HAVE A THRONE, I COULD AT LEAST HAVE *CONTROL* OVER ONE.

"FOR WHEN RODERICK'S QUEEN FELL ILL AND DIED, THE YOUNG PRINCESS MAGDA GREW SULLEN AND REBELLIOUS.

"I KNEW SHE WOULD BE EASILY MANIPULATED. MUCH MORE SO THAN HER ROCK-HEADED FATHER.

"SO I CONCOCTED A PLAN TO PUT *HER* ON THE THRONE.

"IT IS A DELICATE MATTER, THE MURDER OF ONE AS WELL-GUARDED AS A KING.

"IT MUST APPEAR TO BE AN ACCIDENT, OR AT LEAST AS PART OF THE DUE COURSE OF A MONARCH'S BUSINESS.

"THIS IS HOW I CAME TO START THE *FIRST* WAR BETWEEN NORTH HUNTINGTON AND THE NEIGHBORING KINGDOM OF LOTHAR.

"I HAD THE IRON HAND'S AGENTS IN LOTHAR ASSASSINATE A DUKE AND PLANT EVIDENCE THAT NORTH HUNTINGTON WAS TO BLAME.

"THE KINGS OF BOTH NATIONS WERE LIKE COGS IN ONE OF MY MACHINES, DOING EXACTLY AS THEY WERE SUPPOSED TO.

"THE WAR WAS SOON ON.

"BUT THEN RODERICK THREW A WRENCH INTO MY CAREFULLY CRAFTED WORKINGS.

"AS HE LEFT KINGSBRIDGE TO LEAD HIS TROOPS IN WHAT WAS TO BECOME A SIX-YEAR CAMPAIGN, RODERICK HANDED ME A SEALED ENVELOPE.

"I WAS INSTRUCTED TO OPEN IT ONLY IF I RECEIVED WORD HE'D BEEN KILLED.

"THAT'S HOW MUCH THE *FOOL* TRUSTED ME.

"NATURALLY, I READ IT BEFORE HE'D CLEARED THE FIRST HILL.

"IN THE LETTER, RODERICK INFORMED ME THAT SINCE THE DEATH OF THE QUEEN, HE'D BEEN INVOLVED IN A ROMANTIC RELATIONSHIP WITH A WOMAN.

"A WOMAN HE COULDN'T BRING TO COURT BECAUSE SHE WAS A COMMONER...

"...AND BECAUSE HE WAS AFRAID OF HOW MAGDA MIGHT REACT.

"RODERICK HAD BEEN PROVIDING FOR THE WOMAN SECRETLY, AND I WAS TO CONTINUE TO PROVIDE FOR HER IN THE EVENT OF HIS DEATH.

"WITHOUT REALIZING IT, THE KING HAD GIVEN ME THE VERY SECRET TO MANIPULATING HIS DAUGHTER, SERVED AS IF ON A PLATTER.

"WHEN THE TIME WAS RIGHT, I SHOWED THE LETTER TO MAGDA. HER REACTION WAS...

"...AS RODERICK PREDICTED.

"SHE INSISTED ON SEEING THE WOMAN FOR HERSELF.

...NOT UNTIL YOU AND YOUR TWO FRIENDS WERE CAPTURED DURING THAT ILL-ADVISED HEIST ATTEMPT IN THE TREASURE TOWER.

WHEN YOU BEGAN LOUDLY ACCUSING ME OF JARED'S ABDUCTION, I HOPED TO SILENCE YOU QUICKLY...

"...BUT THAT PERPETUALLY BLEEDING HEART, CAPTAIN DRAKE, INSISTED I TAKE YOU BEFORE THE QUEEN...

"...AND MAGDA FINALLY REALIZED THAT I WAS PLOTTING AGAINST HER."

BECAUSE YOUR BROTHER WAS NEVER SUPPOSED TO HAVE LIVED.

"MY PLANS FOR THE KING HAD NOT COME TO FRUITION.

"HE HAD RETURNED FROM WAR, VICTORIOUS AND UNHARMED, AND WAS NO DOUBT SOON TO LEARN THAT HE NOW HAD A MALE HEIR.

"SO MAGDA, FEARFUL OF LOSING HER PLACE IN THE LINE OF SUCCESSION, ORDERED ME TO MURDER THE BOY.

"I QUICKLY AGREED. I PUT DRAKE IN CHARGE OF THE PALACE AND TOOK THE REST OF THE KING'S DRAGONS WITH ME.

"FOR HAVING ALL BUT ONE OF RODERICK'S PERSONAL BODYGUARDS OUT OF THE PALACE COINCIDED NICELY WITH THE MORE....*DIRECT* ARRANGEMENTS THAT I'D ALREADY MADE FOR HIS DEATH."

FOUND HIM, SIR!

"I HAD EVERY INTENTION OF CARRYING OUT MAGDA'S PLAN THAT NIGHT.

"AND YET....

"AT THE LAST MOMENT, I FOUND MYSELF FEELING SOME COMPASSION FOR THE BOY.

"LIKE MYSELF, HE WAS BEING CHEATED OUT OF A KINGDOM THAT WAS RIGHTFULLY HIS.

"USING KINGSBRIDGE GOLD, MY BROTHER RYLAN HAD ALREADY BEGUN CONSTRUCTION OF ASTAROTH, WHICH HAD BEEN INTENDED AS A HIDEOUT FOR IRON HAND ASSASSINS....

All is in readiness. Proceed as planned.

"SO I SWIFTLY DEVISED A BETTER USE FOR OUR HIDDEN ISLAND.

"I WOULD KEEP JARED HIDDEN THERE, TO BE USED AS COLLATERAL IF MAGDA EVER RESISTED MY CONTROL.

"BUT THEN A RARE THING HAPPENED. I WAS OUTSMARTED.

"JARED SNEAKED AWAY AS I WAS HANDING HIM OFF TO RYLAN, WHO WAS TO TAKE HIM TO ASTAROTH."

GOD'S TEETH!

THE BOAT!

"IT WAS BUT A MINOR SETBACK.

"NOW THAT I HAD BEGUN TO THINK OF ASTAROTH IN THIS NEW WAY, I TURNED MY MIND TO WHOM *ELSE* I COULD IMPRISON THERE.

"MAGDA HAD ALWAYS KEPT HER FATHER'S LETTER HIDDEN, EVEN FROM ME.

"FEARING SHE MIGHT ONE DAY USE IT TO BLACKMAIL ME FOR JARED'S APPARENT MURDER, I DID WHATEVER I COULD TO GET IT BACK.

"TO NO AVAIL.

"SO I DISPATCHED THE IRON HAND, WHO KIDNAPPED THE CROWN PRINCE OF LOTHAR, MAKING SURE THAT NORTH HUNTINGTON GOT THE BLAME ONCE AGAIN.

"I HOPED ANOTHER WAR WOULD ENSUE. ONE THAT WOULD MEAN THE END OF MAGDA.

"BUT THE LOTHARS FEARED SIR DRAKE, THE ONLY ONE OF THE QUEEN'S DRAGONS WHO WAS BEYOND MY INFLUENCE, AND WHOM MAGDA KEPT CLOSE FOR THAT VERY REASON.

"IT OCCURRED TO ME THAT IF *ONE* ROYAL HEIR GAVE US POWER, CAPTURING *OTHERS* WOULD GIVE US CONSIDERABLY MORE.

"SO IT BEGAN... A YEARS-LONG ENDEAVOR TO BRING TO ASTAROTH A YOUNG MEMBER OF THE ROYAL FAMILY OF EACH OF THE SIX KINGDOMS.

"THE QUEEN'S DRAGONS AND THE IRON HAND, BOTH NOW UNDER MY COMMAND, WERE INSTRUMENTAL IN THIS.

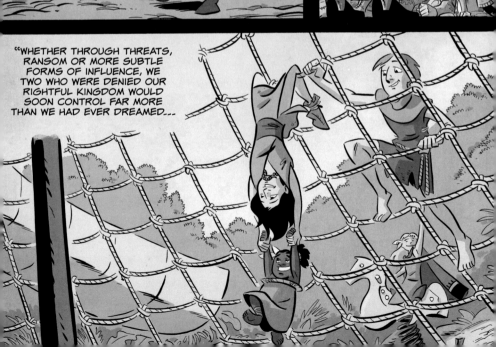

"WHETHER THROUGH THREATS, RANSOM OR MORE SUBTLE FORMS OF INFLUENCE, WE TWO WHO WERE DENIED OUR RIGHTFUL KINGDOM WOULD SOON CONTROL FAR MORE THAN WE HAD EVER DREAMED....

89

...ALL YOU NEED IS THE BEST THIEF IN NORTH HUNTINGTON!

TOPPER!

I WAS AFRAID YOU'D BEEN CAPTURED—OR WORSE!

PFFT...

I'M FAR TOO CRAFTY A WARRIOR TO BE TAKEN DOWN BY A MERE WALL OF ARMED GUARDS.

WHICH IS TO SAY I HID IN A DRAIN UNTIL THE FIGHTING MOVED TO ANOTHER PART OF THE CASTLE.

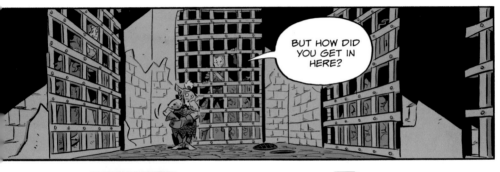

93

KLANK

DESSA_

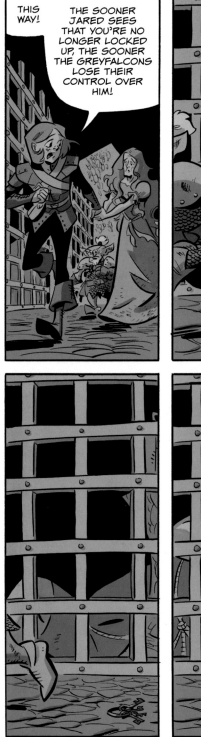

97

SOMEWHERE SAFE.

WHERE SHE WON'T BE HARMED—SO LONG AS THIS WHELP DOES OUR BIDDING.

I SEE.

THEN YOU MEAN TO LEVERAGE HER AGAINST THE THRONE, AS YOU ONCE DID ME.

I WON'T HAVE IT.

NOR WILL I.

UNTIL **THIS** WEIGHT WAS PUT ON MY HEAD, I WAS A SIMPLE STABLE BOY, RAISED BY HONEST, HARDWORKING FOLK.

I'D DO ANYTHING TO RETURN TO THAT LIFE.

KING OLIVAR, YOU HAVE BESTED THE ARMIES OF NORTH HUNTINGTON, AND PROVEN YOURSELF A BRAVE AND NOBLE LEADER...

100

101

THIS BOY IS KING RODERICK'S FIRSTBORN SON.

THE CROWN IS *HIS ALONE.*

LONG MAY HE WEAR IT. AND LONG MAY HE ALLOW ME TO SERVE HIM AS MY KING.

I...

105

107

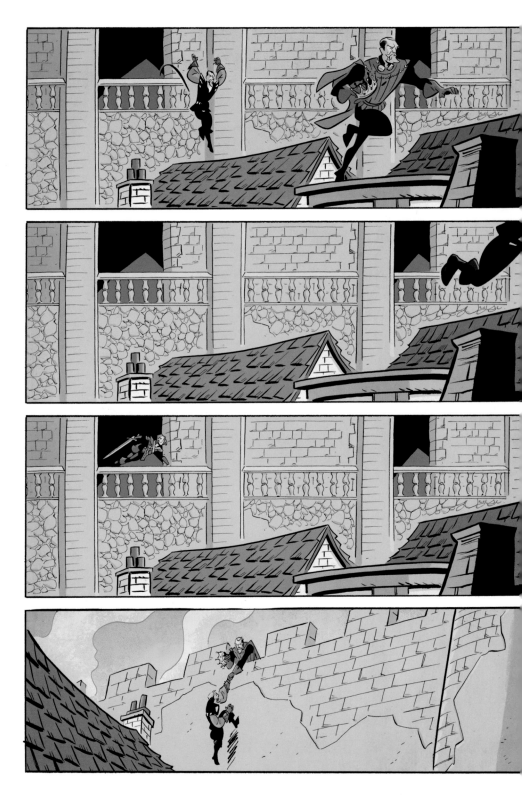

HEY, GREYFALCONS!

SLICE

SPLASH

114

Epilogue

HE WOULD, BLESS HIM. EVEN AFTER ALL THESE YEARS, I BELIEVE HE'D STILL DO ANYTHING FOR DESSA.

THE MEDORIANS WON'T BE THERE QUICKLY ENOUGH...

WE'LL NEED TO SEND WARNING TO EVERY TOWN AND VILLAGE NORTH OF THE RIVER.

SEND OUT ONE OF THE DRAGONS. OUR FASTEST RIDER.

THEIR CAPTAIN, THEN.

THREE THIEVES

Don't miss any of the Three Thieves adventures!

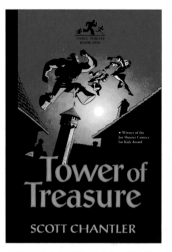

HC 978-1-55453-414-2 • $17.95
PB 978-1-55453-415-9 • $7.95

HC 978-1-55453-416-6 • $17.95
PB 978-1-55453-417-3 • $8.95

HC 978-1-55453-776-1 • $17.95
PB 978-1-55453-777-8 • $8.95

HC 978-1-55453-778-5 • $17.95
PB 978-1-55453-779-2 • $8.95

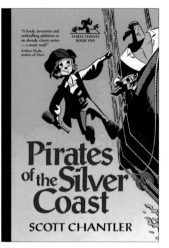

HC 978-1-894786-53-9 • $17.95
PB 978-1-894786-54-6 • $8.95

HC 978-1-894786-55-3 • $16.95
PB 978-1-894786-56-0 • $7.95